Why
do people
Gamble?

Kaye Stearman

an imprint of Hodder Children's Books

© 2000 White-Thomson Publishing Ltd

Produced for Hodder Wayland by
White-Thomson Publishing Ltd
2/3 St Andrew's Place
Lewes
BN7 1UP

A Catalogue record for this book is available
from the British Library.

ISBN 07502 2764 8

Printed and bound in Italy
by G. Canale & C.S.p.A., Turin.

Hodder Children's Books
A division of Hodder Headline Limited
338 Euston Road
London NW1 3BH

Series concept: Alex Woolf
Editor: Liz Gogerly
Cover Design: Hodder Children's Books
Inside Design: Mark Whitchurch Art & Design
Consultant: Paul Bellringer of GAMCARE
Picture Research: Gina Brown - Glass Onion
      Pictures
Proofreader: Alison Cooper
Indexer: Jackie Butterley

Picture acknowledgements

The publisher would like to thank the following for
their kind permission to use their pictures:
Eye Ubiquitous/ Dean Bennett 12 (bottom)/
Paul Seheult 20/ Craig Hutchins 32;
Ronald Grant Archive 25 (bottom);
Robert Harding 19 (top); Hodder Wayland Picture
Library (imprint page), 12 (top), 12, 14, 21, 30/
Chris Fairclough 31/ Dorian Shaw 19 (bottom), 38;
Impact/ Peter Arkell 24, 44/ Lionel Derimais 18/
Alain Evrard 15 (bottom)/ Alain le Garsmeur 26/
Robert Gibbs 6 (top)/ Jared A Jafferji 8/
Trevor Morgan 10/ Simon Shepherd 40/
Daniel White 17; Newens 5, 7;
Popperfoto 4 (bottom), 11, 22, 23, 27, 29, 41, 42,
43, 45; Chris Schwarz (contents)(top), 36;
Tony Stone (cover), (contents) (bottom), 4 (top), 6
(bottom), 16, 23, 28, 35; The Stock Market 25 (top).

Cover picture: money spilling out of a fruit machine

Contents

1 What is gambling?

What do you think gambling is?

When you think of gambling what picture comes into your mind? Do you think of somebody losing all their money on a horse? Or somebody playing cards for fun in a casino? Do you imagine somebody feeding coins into a fruit machine and winning lots of money? Perhaps you think of making a bet with a friend on which team will win a football game? Or maybe you picture somebody scooping millions in the lottery?

▲ A group of friends enjoy a pot of tea and a game of cards in China.

◀ One in a million – a winning lottery ticket has brought this family wealth and changed their lives for ever.

These are all ways of gambling – and many of us come into contact with gambling every day. For most people, gambling is a small and enjoyable part of their life. Some people decide that gambling is not for them at all so it hardly affects their lives. But for a few people, gambling takes over their lives and they become hooked.

But what is gambling? In short, gambling involves risking something you value (usually money) in the hope that you will be better off afterwards. Risk means that you take a chance – you might win or you might lose or you might end up exactly the same. The bigger the risk, the bigger the winnings or losses will be. If the risk is small, then the winnings or losses will be small.

'Games of chance' are activities where the result depends on chance and is not influenced by a person's skill. Examples include rolling dice, picking a playing card or buying a scratch card. However, not all gambling involves games of chance. Some skill or knowledge may be involved. When people play a card game, like poker, or place a bet on a horse-race or football match, no one knows what the result will be. However, a skilful or knowledgeable person has a better chance of getting the right result.

> 'In play there are two pleasures for your choosing;
> The one is winning and the other losing.'
> Don Juan, *Lord Byron*.

Amusement arcades offer many chances to gamble – some people spend hours playing the machines.

Different kinds of gambling

There are three main types of gambling:

gaming – playing games of chance or skill for money, including card games (poker, blackjack, etc.), wheel games (such as roulette) or on special machines (fruit machines, electronic gaming machines)

betting – placing money on the result of an event, such as a sports meeting (horse-racing, athletics, football)

lotteries – buying a ticket or a scratch card with a chance to win a prize

▲ *Betting on horse-racing is one of the most popular kinds of gambling.*

The word gambling is very close to the word 'game'. The idea of a game is very important in gambling. A game is (or should be):

active – an agreed activity happens

limited – action takes place over an agreed time or distance

rule-bound – everyone knows and follows the rules

fair – there is no cheating or bad behaviour

unpredictable – no one knows the result in advance

▼ *A roulette game on a city street in Colombia, South America.*

Sometimes, people feel that the game is more important than the result – winning or losing. Perhaps it is because people like to play games that gambling is so popular.

case study · case study · case study · case study · case study

Kirsty doesn't gamble – or does she? At age fifteen, the law says she is too young to buy lottery tickets or bet on horses. If you ask her parents, they will say that of course she doesn't gamble – she is too young and, anyway, they would know about it.

If you talk to Kirsty privately she might admit that she buys lottery tickets and scratch cards. Shopkeepers are not supposed to sell them to young people but some do, especially if the customer looks older than he or she really is.

But, actually, Kirsty finds the lottery rather boring. Unusually, for a girl, she prefers to hang out at the amusement arcade, playing the fruit machines. Kirsty enjoys the atmosphere – noise, flashing lights, bright colours. Above all, she likes the fact that her parents don't know she is there.

Maybe, one day, the fruit machines will lose their excitement for Kirsty. Perhaps she will discover other things, like clothes, clubbing or boys. Or maybe she will discover new types of gambling. What do you think?

▶ *Many young people find the amusement arcade an exciting place to hang out.*

What is luck?

'Win some, lose some.' 'It's a sure bet.' 'A bird in the hand is worth two in the bush.' 'Easy come, easy go.' 'I feel lucky today.' 'My luck is about to change.' 'She's so lucky you wouldn't believe it.' 'He just keeps beating the odds.' We have all heard expressions like these. There are many reasons why a person can be considered lucky, but, in gambling, a lucky person is a winner – someone who beats the odds.

But what is luck and how does it work? And are some people really more lucky than others? In games of chance, luck depends on mathematical rules, called the laws of probability. They tell us how often something is likely to happen by calculating the mathematical chances (odds) that it will happen.

> "
> Simon Trumper, a top poker player, parks his car on a double yellow line. 'Once in 15 times I'll be caught. I think that's good odds. I like to take risks.'
> The Financial Times, 22 April 2000.
> "

▼ Boys gather around a gambling table, at a travelling fair in Zanzibar, East Africa.

activity · activity · activity

Take a six-sided die, with each side having between one and six dots. What is the chance of throwing a six? The answer is 1 in 6. What is the chance of throwing another six? Again, it is 1 in 6. There is the same 1 in 6 chance on the third throw. Every throw has the same chance as any other throw.

What is the chance of throwing 2 sixes in a row? You need to multiply the chances: first 1 x 6, then another 1 x 6 (6 x 6). The answer is 1 in 36. The chance of throwing 3 sixes in a row is even less likely – only 1 in 216 (6 x 6 x 6).

The die is a very simple example. Most odds are much more difficult to calculate. Probability is based on complex statistics, often running into millions of different combinations of numbers. Today, scientists can use high-powered computers to work out the odds on almost anything – even something like whether a huge meteor will crash into the earth.

In gambling, luck is when you beat the mathematical odds. In real life, people can, and do, have 'runs of luck', when everything seems to go their way. But in the end, the laws of probability mean that no person can be lucky for too long.

▶ *Studying the form guide before placing a bet on the Kentucky Derby, the USA's most famous horse-race.*

Gambling – past and present

Gambling is not new. We can find many examples of people gambling throughout history, in different countries and cultures all over the world. Gambling has been part of people's lives for a long time.

One of the commonest forms of gambling is betting, which is placing money on the result of an event, usually to decide who is the fastest, strongest or toughest. Two thousand years ago, in ancient Rome, thousands of people bet on the horse-races held in the huge Circus Maximus. Betting was well-organized. Each horse belonged to a team known by their colours – the Blues, Greens, Whites and so on. Spectators put money on their favourite teams, receiving bone disks in return. Gamblers could cash in the disks if their horse won. But, just like today, most people only bet small sums and enjoyed the fun of a day out.

> 'Twas I won the wager, though you hit the white; And being a winner, God give you good night!'
> Taming of the Shrew, *William Shakespeare.*

◀ *A village cockfight in Bali, Indonesia. The cocks spend months in training but fights may be over in seconds.*

▲ *A French goal in the 1998 football World Cup final. Most betting went on a Brazilian win but the French team won 3-0.*

However, most betting takes place on a smaller scale, often among people who know each other well. On the Indonesian island of Bali, people bet on fights between specially trained fighting cocks. Two birds, with sharp spurs strapped on to their legs, face each other in a small space. The excited audience place their bets. Sometimes, a village will place a large bet on their favourite. Fights rarely last long – sometimes just a few seconds – but they cause great excitement.

Betting goes well beyond sporting events. The fact is that people will bet on anything – and often do! What will be the next card in the pack, whether there will be snow on Christmas Day, who will win the next election, and much more.

Lotteries and how they work

Lotteries are a common form of gambling. In a lottery, many people buy tickets. The money collected from the tickets goes towards the prizes. The winning ticket is chosen at random, with every ticket having an equal chance of winning. Lotteries are often seen as the most acceptable form of gambling because ticket prices are low and the risks are small.

Like betting, lotteries have a long history. Many governments have organized lotteries to help raise money for grand buildings or government services. Lotteries are also a popular way of raising money for good causes, like charities, sports or the arts. The famous Sydney Opera House was built with lottery money.

▼ *A lottery in nineteenth-century Britain.*

▼ *You can find lotteries almost everywhere. This man sells lottery tickets in Kerala, southern India.*

> 'But the lottery isn't really gambling, is it? I mean, you aren't really risking anything and you might win.'
> *Jack, 16, USA.*

case study · case study · case study · case study · case study

Each week, Steve's family buys three tickets in the UK National Lottery. One ticket always has the same set of 'lucky' numbers based upon family birthdays. Steve and his sister help to choose the numbers on the other tickets.

Everyone watches the Saturday draw on television. Sometimes, several numbers match the winning combination – one ticket won over £100 and everyone was thrilled. But no ticket has ever got near the big prize.

Steve takes the Lottery very seriously. He dreams about what a big win would mean – a new house, fast cars, great holidays, lots of games. His parents are much less serious – they know the odds of winning the jackpot are one in 14 million.

▶ *Waiting around the television for the results of the UK National Lottery – maybe this will be their lucky week.*

In Spain, the lottery is known as 'El Gordo' – 'the fat one' – because the prizes are so large. When the UK National Lottery began in 1994, some people thought there would be little interest. In fact, millions of people buy Lottery tickets each week.

Is gambling allowed?

Gambling has often been controversial, disliked and feared by many people. Therefore, gambling often occurred at times and places known only to a few people. Until fairly recently, many types of gambling were against the law in most countries. As a result, most gambling took place behind closed doors and was often controlled by criminals.

Eventually, some governments passed laws to allow different types of gambling. They hoped that if gambling was made a legal business, like any other, then criminals would no longer be involved. In many countries, governments allowed betting shops to be set up for horse-racing and other sporting events, and casinos for gambling on card games or roulette.

▲ *Al Capone made money from criminal activities and gambling in the USA in the 1920s.*

FACT:
The popular television programme *Who Wants To Be a Millionaire* has been banned in Sweden by television authorities. It was felt that the programme was more like a lottery than a game of skill and therefore needed a special licence to be shown on television.
Lottery.co.uk, February 2000.

As legal gambling became more established, many governments realized that they could increase their income by placing heavy taxes on the gambling industry. They saw that gambling could attract tourists and provide jobs for local people. As a result, there was a huge increase in the gambling industry and the opportunities for gambling.

▲ *Las Vegas, USA, by night – the greatest gambling venue ever.*

In the USA, the city of Las Vegas, in the state of Nevada, rapidly grew into the gambling capital of the world. Huge casinos offering card games and roulette tables operated around the clock. The introduction of electronic gaming machines – slot machines or poker machines – attracted even more people. Casinos built huge hotels and provided glamorous entertainment and cheap food and drink. Each year, millions of tourists continue to come to Las Vegas to have fun and gamble. Nearly all lose their money.

▶ *This local casino in the Philippines is illegal. It is very different from Las Vegas but the gambling is just as exciting.*

2. How is gambling changing?

Gambling on the increase

Gambling is on the increase all around the world. One reason is that many people have more money than in the past. They also have more leisure time so they look for ways to spend their money and fill their time. Some people seek thrills and excitement, others look for something relaxing. Gambling can be sociable and a way of meeting people; it can also be done alone. Gambling fits in to different lifestyles and is enjoyed in many ways.

Gambling has also increased in most countries as attitudes towards gambling have become more open and relaxed. Governments often look to gambling to provide jobs and income from taxes. Gambling provides lots of new business opportunities, not just for gambling itself but for spin-off businesses providing food, drink and entertainment.

▼ *A camel-race in a Middle Eastern country. Some people like the excitement, others come to bet.*

Compared to the past, people have more opportunities to gamble. There are now many different places dedicated to gambling, ranging from basic betting shops to plush casinos. At the same time, new technology has resulted in new types of gambling. Computers and the Internet mean that gambling can take place in cyberspace, 24 hours a day.

Places for gambling include:
  casinos
  clubs, bars, pubs and hotels
  betting shops
  race courses
  sports grounds
  cyberspace, through the Internet

FACT:
Between 1975 and 1997 income from legal gambling in the USA grew by 1,600 per cent.
National Gambling Impact Study, June 1999.

Some people feel that there are now too many opportunities for gambling. They say that gambling has moved from being an occasional activity for a few people to being a regular part of daily life for millions. In fact, some people go so far as to say that the world faces an explosion of gambling.

▶ *Betting on a bug! People bet on fighting beetles in northern Thailand.*

Gambling in a modern world

Once, nearly all gambling took place face to face. Today, most gambling takes place at a distance. Technologies such as telephones, radio and television have changed the way people gamble. A gambler can place bets by telephone, listen to race meetings or sporting events on the radio or watch them on television. Cable television has brought viewers hundreds of channels. Satellites bounce news and sport across the world. People can view events thousands of kilometres away, while relaxing at home.

> **FACT:**
> In early 2000 there were more than 650 websites offering many types of gambling. In 1999, on-line gambling income was $1.2 billion, this is likely to grow to more than $3 billion in 2002.
> **The Financial Times, April 2000**

▼ *A solitary gambler considers his bet while screens flash the latest odds, races and results.*

Today, the newest forms of gambling take place in cyberspace via the Internet. Instead of visiting casinos, clubs or race-tracks, or ringing bookmakers or betting shops, gamblers use a computer to log on to special websites where they can play a game or make a bet on-line. Rather than go to a real casino, club or race-track, and gamble with real people, the gambler uses virtual casinos, virtual lotteries and virtual sports betting. No longer are they gambling on real events but on computer-generated activities. But they still have to use real money, usually through a credit card.

▲ *The betting shop is just a phone call away. Now, gamblers can use on-line betting too.*

Cyberspace crosses time zones and country borders. For example, someone in Australia can gamble at a virtual casino owned by a company based on an island in the Caribbean. And they can gamble or play at any hour of the day or night.

▼ *The Internet can be used for education, for fun and for gambling.*

Some experts think that the Internet will be the future of gambling. Others are not so sure. They point out that Internet gambling can be very lonely and cannot substitute for the excitement of real gambling with real people.

The rise of the scratch card

Computer technology has contributed to another popular form of gambling – the scratch card. These are stiff paper tickets produced in batches of millions. Each ticket has a number combination, generated by a computer. The combination is revealed when the ticket surface is scratched with a coin or sharp object. Some combinations win a small cash prize. The rarest combinations bring much larger amounts. Most tickets turn out to be worthless.

Scratch cards are a special sort of lottery. In a regular lottery, players have to wait until the draw takes place. With a scratch card, the result is known as soon as the card is scratched. Some people say this is why scratch cards are so popular – winners get an instant buzz. Today, scratch cards are found all over the world. They are proving popular with young people because they are cheap and easy to use.

▼ *In many countries, you can buy a lottery ticket or scratch card from a street seller, like this trader in Sri Lanka.*

case study · case study · case study · case study · case study

'Kwacha Mania!!!' is a familiar phrase in Zambia. These are the words displayed on Perton's yellow booth and on his tee-shirt. Perton sells scratch cards in Lusaka, the capital of Zambia.

Each morning, Perton displays rows of brightly coloured cards in the booth. It's a busy area and sales are steady. He sells to shoppers and office workers, market traders and truck drivers. Anyone can buy a card, even young children. Some people scratch their cards immediately; others wait till later. Some buy them regularly, others only occasionally.

Scratch cards are very popular in Zambia, even though it's a poor country and money is tight. The cards are known as *fwenya fwenya* – 'scratch scratch' in the Bemba language. Each card costs 1,000 kwacha and prizes range from 2,000 kwacha to 25 million kwacha. Whenever a customer wins a prize, Perton hopes that their luck will rub off on him.

Note: Zambia's currency is the kwacha. In January 2000, 1,000 kwacha was worth about 25 pence.

◄ A used scratch card from Zambia, Africa. As you can see, there was no prize for this particular card.

3. Why do people gamble?

Reasons people gamble

"

'Everybody gambles sometimes. You don't want to be left out, do you?' *Lillian, 22.*

'My parents gamble. They buy lottery tickets every week.' *Sam, 14.*

'If you do win, you get rich and everyone looks up to you.' *Jack, 12.*

'Betting can be fun.' *Graham, 44.*

'I enjoy playing the fruit machines, especially if there's a group of us.' *Philip, 15.*

'Some people just can't stop gambling. They try but they can't give it up.' *George, 23.*

'You get a buzz when you win.' *Mark, 27.*

'It's all about winning, isn't it? You never know when your luck is going to change.' *Leslie, 36.*

"

As we have seen, people have been gambling for a long time, while today there are more opportunities to gamble than ever before. But this doesn't explain why people gamble.

▼ *Hoping to strike it lucky, a Chinese man searches the pavement for a winning scratch card.*

People gamble for any of the reasons below:
- it's an enjoyable hobby
- to mix with other people
- to gain status
- to get a buzz
- to win money
- to recover lost money
- to earn a living
- out of desperation
- it's an addiction

The fact is that there are many reasons why people gamble. Often, gambling plays a small part in people's lives and, for these people, gambling is an interesting, enjoyable way of relaxing – just like any other hobby. Gambling can also be extremely exciting and many gamblers get a buzz out of winning. For them, gambling is like skiing or surfing, where the thrill of the moment is more important than the risks involved.

For some gamblers, winning is very important. They enjoy winning money but they may also win status. People look up to a winner, especially if they have special knowledge or skill. Again, most people gamble small amounts of money. They stay in control of their gambling, and it rarely results in problems for themselves or others.

▲ *A record jackpot winner in Las Vegas, USA. In 1997, the lady on the left won $125 million in a slot machine.*

◀ *You are never too old to gamble and to enjoy the thrill of winning.*

Gambling for fun

Gambling is often seen as a social activity. For example, friends might go on a night out to a horse-race or dog track. They go out to gamble but the main reason for going is to mix with their friends. Workmates regularly join together to buy lottery tickets – being part of a team is as important as winning. Sometimes, groups of people hold a sweepstake.

A sweepstake is where a group of people put money on a horse-race or a football tournament, for example. Each person is given a certain horse or team, and the person with the winning horse or team wins all the money put on the race or match by the group. Winning the sweepstake might not be as important as the fun of joining in the game.

▶ *Bingo is a popular and sociable way to gamble, especially among older people.*

► A day at Royal Ascot is a fun day out and an opportunity to bet on a winning horse.

Often gambling is just part of a big day out. Famous race-meetings, such as Royal Ascot in the UK or the Kentucky Derby in the USA, have special days when women dress in beautiful clothes and hats. These events are expensive and it can be difficult to get tickets. Some people only go to have a small bet, or 'flutter', on the horses. The most important part of their day is being seen by the right people in the right place.

Films and television have also made gambling appear fun and an easy way to make money. Films show down-on-their-luck card players winning lots of money. James Bond often appears in casinos – he usually wins and he often meets beautiful women there. These kinds of image help to make gambling seem exciting and glamorous.

► James Bond, the fictitious superspy, dresses in a dinner suit when he visits a casino.

Professional gamblers

Every gambler wants to win. Sometimes, a gambler is lucky but most lose far more money than they win. Most gamblers know when to stop but some become desperate. Even when they are losing heavily, they keep playing, hoping that their luck will change.

A few people earn their living from gambling, mainly by playing games of skill in clubs and casinos. If they become too successful, a club may ban them, so they move from place to place. But even professional gamblers lose money.

Some people become addicted to gambling, in the same way as people become addicted to alcohol or drugs. For addicts, gambling is an end in itself. Of course, they enjoy winning but, even if they win, they gamble away their winnings. An addict does not care about family or friendship or building up social ties or gaining status. Gambling is much more than fun or excitement. Without gambling, their life would not be worth living.

▼ *Far from the glamorous crowds, an anxious gambler studies the odds at Royal Ascot races.*

case study · case study · case study

Al is a professional gambler – he makes his living playing poker in clubs and casinos all over the world. Few people have Al's skill or steely nerves. But you wouldn't notice Al in a crowded room – he tries not to draw attention to himself.

▼ *A professional gambler will travel the world playing in clubs and casinos.*

The main source of Al's income are 'suckers', people who start off gambling for fun and then get sucked in. Al looks for a sucker and then deliberately lets them win a few games. The sucker feels lucky and risks more money. Then Al moves in.

Al has been a gambler most of his life. Over the years, he has won and lost more money than most people earn in a lifetime. For Al, gambling is like any demanding job – it takes constant practice, hard work and long hours. Anyway, after so long, he couldn't really do anything else.

4. What is problem gambling?

How does problem gambling start?

Some people become addicted to gambling. They cannot stop gambling, even when they have lost all their money. Their whole life revolves around their habit. The term 'problem gambling' is used when a person has become addicted to gambling. Their addiction to gambling causes harm to themselves and to their family, and may also affect the wider community.

Addiction is not easy to understand. No one knows why some people become addicted to gambling while others do not. But we do not need to understand why people become addicted to gambling to be able to understand the real difficulties that problem gambling can create for gamblers and the people around them.

▲ Gamblers struggle to place their bets at a race course in Vietnam.

Problem gambling creates huge financial and personal difficulties for the gambler. First, the gambler gambles away their income. Then they draw on their savings or use their credit cards.

Next, they might sell their property or re-mortgage their home. They might borrow money from family or friends who may not realize that the money is used for gambling. Often they find the only people who will lend them money are 'loan sharks' – moneylenders who charge very high rates of interest (although this is against the law in many countries).

Finally, the gambler may turn to crime, especially to so-called 'white collar crime', such as stealing from employers or customers. Many gamblers also steal from family members, although these cases are not often reported to the police.

▲ *Excitement and disappointment for two young women at this lottery in China. This is low-risk gambling.*

FACT:
Worldwide, men and boys are more likely to gamble than women and girls. In some countries, it is not socially acceptable for women to gamble, at least in public. Where women do gamble, they tend to go for low-risk gambling, like lotteries or bingo. Men generally have more money for gambling and they are more likely to be high-risk gamblers, betting on horses, sporting events or cards, or playing slot machines. Men are also more likely to develop problems with gambling.

What are the effects of problem gambling?

Losing money is only one of the difficulties facing a problem gambler. Much worse are the feelings they experience of guilt, shame and depression. Most problem gamblers keep these feelings bottled up inside rather than sharing them and, in the end, because they cannot ask for help, this usually makes their problems even worse.

Here are the main problem areas and some of the difficulties that might result:

♦ money problems – increasing debt and financial stress, leading to loss of home and property, borrowing from loan sharks, involvement in criminal activity, arrest and trial, prison

♦ emotional problems – feelings of guilt, shame and anxiety, leading to depression, alcohol and drug addiction, attempted suicide

♦ relationship problems – lying and dishonesty (especially about money) with family, friends and workmates, leading to lack of trust, arguments, violence, abuse, stealing, break-ups with family and friends

▼ *Despair, depression and shame are common feelings when someone is addicted to gambling.*

♦ school and work problems – taking time off, resulting in truancy, dropping out of school, losing jobs, long-term unemployment

▲ *Problem gambling can cause relationships to break up – children suffer as well as adults.*

Problem gambling goes far beyond the gambler to affect the people around them. Problem gamblers frequently borrow or steal money from family, friends and workmates. They may intend to return the money – and sometimes do – but mostly it just gets gambled away. It is hard to trust a person if they constantly steal, cheat and lie.

Surveys have found each problem gambler affects the lives of many other people. These include:
♦ family members
♦ friends and neighbours
♦ employers, employees and workmates
♦ creditors – people who are owed money

'A compulsive gambler will bet until nothing is left: savings, family assets, personal belongings anything that can be pawned, sold or borrowed against. In desperation, they turn to crime.'
Australia's Gambling Industries report, 1999.

Stopping the gambling habit

Most problem gamblers find it extremely hard to break their gambling habit. It usually takes several years for a gambler to recognize the harm caused by gambling, and take action to stop.

It is so easy for a problem gambler to think: 'Just one more game... just one win and then I'll stop.' In practice, one more game turns into another and another. For this reason, groups such as Gamblers Anonymous say that a problem gambler must stop gambling and never gamble again.

FACT:
Gamblers Anonymous started in Los Angeles, California, in 1957 when problem gamblers began meeting regularly in an attempt to stop gambling. There are now similar groups all over the world. All members must have a genuine desire to stop gambling and give support and encouragement to each other.

Nevertheless, regular, addictive gambling is a habit that can be broken. There are different ways to achieve this but they all take a lot of time, effort and determination.

▼ *A problem gambler may live in their own world and not care about others.*

case study · case study · case study · case study · case study

Astrid lives in New Jersey with her daughter Christine. Until recently, Astrid went out most evenings, leaving Christine alone at home. Astrid had a regular job – yet money just slipped through her fingers. Bills went unpaid and the telephone and electricity were cut off. Sometimes, there was no food in the house.

Most of Astrid's income went on gambling. She had started gambling soon after her divorce. She was so lonely and the casino seemed warm and safe. She loved the crowded rooms, the smoke and the lights. Above all, she loved the buzz she got when she was winning.

One day, she returned home and found Christine crying, hungry and frightened in the darkened house. Something snapped and Astrid had to admit she was hooked on gambling. For Christine's sake, she had to stop. A few days later, she attended her first meeting of Gamblers Anonymous.

▶ *Some people find gambling a retreat from the real world of stress and worry.*

5. Why can't children gamble?

▲ Never too young to gamble – or are they? These boys in India have begun gambling early in life.

The reasons why children shouldn't gamble

The law treats children differently from adults. Children cannot vote in government elections or sign business contracts or get a driving licence. Most countries have laws forbidding children to buy and smoke cigarettes, buy and drink alcohol in public, or gamble for money. Children are not allowed into areas where gambling takes place, such as casinos, clubs or betting shops, even if they are with their parents.

Here are some of the reasons given for keeping children away from gambling activities.

♦ gambling (like cigarettes and alcohol) can cause harm to bodies and minds, particularly to young, growing bodies and minds. Children cannot fully appreciate how harmful gambling can be, so they need special protection

♦ gambling can be addictive. What we learn in childhood affects the rest of our life. Many problem gamblers develop gambling habits early in life

♦ gambling, whether placing a bet or buying a lottery ticket, requires a clear understanding of the risks involved. Children do not understand risks properly (and nor do many adults)

FACT:
Millions of children regularly use computers to access the Internet, to search websites, to send e-mails and play games. Some people fear that children might find some of the many gambling websites and begin to gamble on-line, using stolen credit cards. Others say that this is unlikely, that most children are too interested in the other exciting things the Internet has to offer to bother about gambling.

♦ gambling needs money. Most children do not have money of their own (apart from pocket money). Children who gamble are likely to borrow or steal money from others – usually their parents

♦ gambling normally happens in a place designed for adults, rather than children. For example, there may be adult entertainment, plentiful alcohol, smoking or drugs. This atmosphere is not suitable for children

▼ *Adults gambling in a casino. The law says children are not allowed inside.*

How does gambling affect children?

Problem gambling has a direct impact on children. The most common effects are poverty and neglect. A parent gambles away money that should be spent on food, clothes and housekeeping. Older children may be kept from school to baby-sit younger children while a parent is gambling.

Children also experience emotional problems. One survey from the USA found that 60 per cent of children of problem gamblers had emotional problems. They were moody, withdrawn, angry and depressed. Many had poor grades in school and some played truant or dropped out of school early. Some turned to drugs or alcohol; some even attempted suicide.

'Problem gambling – like other social problems – can cascade down generations. People whose parents had a problem are much more likely to develop a problem themselves.'
Australia's Gambling Industries report, 1999.

▶ *Children's lives are affected by poverty and neglect – a parent's gambling may be a cause of both.*

◀ A small boy is neglected while his father gambles in Japan.

Many problem gamblers try to hide their addiction from their families, and their children are not directly exposed to gambling even though they may be affected by it. When gambling is practised openly, children are likely to pick up gambling habits at an early age. As a result, they are more likely to gamble and to become problem gamblers themselves.

In fact, many problem gamblers become addicted to gambling when they are young – often too young to gamble legally. Many people who go on to develop gambling problems begin gambling between the ages of eight and thirteen – in some cases when they are still at primary school.

Boys seem to enjoy risk taking more than girls do Whatever the reason, boys are much more likely to begin gambling, to continue gambling as they get older and to develop gambling problems.

FACT:
Problem gambling is often a family problem. A study in the UK revealed that one third of problem gamblers had a father who was also a problem gambler.
In the USA, the proportion was about one quarter.
Australia's Gambling Industries report, 1999.

It's your choice

Growing up is about making decisions. As children become teenagers, then adults, they find that they have more decisions to make. Gambling often poses difficult choices for young people. Good information provides a basis for making good decisions.

Here are some questions about gambling that you might like to think about:

Do I want to gamble?

If my friends gamble should I join in, even if I am not keen?

♦ Does the law say I am old enough to gamble?

Is a particular type of gambling legal in my country, state or province?

How do I get information about different types of gambling?

Are some types of gambling safer or less risky than others?

Do I understand the different types of gambling, how they operate and the odds against winning?

Do I know how much money is involved and the risks, especially if I lose?

Can I stop gambling when I decide I have had enough?

Can I recognize problems that might arise from gambling?

▼ *A game of cards with your friends can be fun. If you play for money and lose is it still as much fun though?*

case study · case study · case study · case study · case study

Bill, who lives in Manchester in the UK, thinks he knows a lot about gambling. His father spent most weekends at the local club, playing the poker machines or placing bets on horses. Sometimes he won, mostly he lost. But he was always convinced that a big win was coming his way.

Bill was too young to go to the club or place bets. But, after school, he would head for the local amusement arcade, to play the fruit machines with his mates. All Bill's pocket money went into the machines. He loved the noise, the lights and the excitement. Bill skipped school to spend time at the arcade. Not surprisingly, he fell behind in class.

By the time Bill reached his mid-teens he was gambling regularly. By the time he was old enough to gamble legally, he was hooked – he just couldn't stop gambling.

▶ *Young men are more likely to develop problems with gambling.*

6. Should gambling be banned?

The risks of gambling

Gambling is a subject that many people find confusing and unsettling. They have mixed feelings about gambling. On the one hand, they may gamble themselves, whether regularly or occasionally, and find it interesting and enjoyable. On the other hand, they understand that gambling may create problems for individuals and communities. As more and more people become involved in gambling, the dangers will also grow.

> 'Although it creates no new goods or services, gambling absorbs time and resources.'
> *Paul Samuelson,*
> *Nobel Prize-winning economist.*

As we have seen, gambling poses particular risks because gamblers may:
♦ not understand the rules or the odds
♦ be cheated or duped
♦ lose more than they can afford
♦ develop problems or addictions

◄ *Down and out ... problem gambling may be one reason this man is on the streets.*

The major risk is losing money. In the long run, all gamblers lose money because the odds are against them. But problem gamblers stand to lose much more than money. They can lose their family, friends, house and job, as well as their good name, health and mental well-being.

Some people say that gambling is so risky and dangerous that it should be banned by the government. They point to the growth of the gambling industry and the increasing numbers of problem gamblers. In fact, some governments have tried to ban various forms of gambling. Gamblers, and people who organize gambling, are punished by heavy fines or gaol sentences.

Most religions take a strong stand against some types of gambling, and some religions do not approve of any gambling. For example, practising Jews, Muslims and Methodist Protestants are forbidden to gamble. Some religious groups have provided services to help problem gamblers overcome their addiction.

◀ *Many governments do not like gambling and limit it to government casinos, like this one in the Middle East.*

41

Why is it difficult to ban gambling?

Experience from many countries shows it is extremely difficult to ban gambling altogether. Here are some reasons why.

♦ Most people who gamble do so occasionally, for small amounts of money. Only a small number go on to become problem gamblers. If gambling is banned, it discriminates against most gamblers who do not have problems.

♦ Many people enjoy gambling and want to continue. If some forms of gambling are banned, they will find others. These may be more risky or dangerous than before.

♦ When gambling is banned, the gambling industry doesn't disappear. It continues to operate, secretly and illegally. As a result, gambling falls into the hands of criminals, ranging from local gangs to the Mafia. Gambling becomes more dangerous for everyone. Gamblers have no protection if they are cheated, robbed or beaten up by criminals and loan sharks.

♦ When gambling is legal, governments can lay down rules to ensure fair play for gamblers, and set age limits for children and young people. Governments cannot protect people if gambling is banned.

▼ *Buying lottery tickets in Kentucky, USA. In the USA, people often drive to the next state to gamble if they cannot do so locally.*

♦ The gambling industry, and the people who work in it, are taxed by the government. If gambling is banned, income from these taxes is lost. Governments may have to place higher taxes on other activities and workers.

♦ Profits from some gambling activities, such as government lotteries, go to good causes. If gambling is banned, some good causes would not be funded.

♦ If gambling is banned, police may spend valuable time and resources on tracking down small-time gamblers, while large-scale gambling and other serious crimes are neglected.

♦ Gambling is now an international industry. When gambling is banned in one country, the industry moves to another country. Technology, such as the Internet, allows people to gamble in another country without leaving home.

▲ *The grand opening of the Royal Opera House, London. Money for rebuilding it came from the UK National Lottery.*

Playing safe with gambling

Most governments accept that it is simply not possible to ban all gambling. Instead, they try to ensure fair play and to warn gamblers about the risks of gambling.

Like gambling, many activities are risky or harmful – driving, drinking alcohol, smoking cigarettes, taking hard drugs – even cooking. Many governments try to tell the public about the risks by:

♦ providing information (leaflets, helplines)
  running campaigns (slogans, posters, television adverts)
  passing laws and regulations (speed limits, fines, age limits)

Below are slogans used in public education campaigns in several countries. These slogans, linked with strong images, were used on posters and in television adverts. They aimed to educate people about the risks. They also aimed to shock people, to get them to stop behaving recklessly and act more carefully.

  Hot water burns like fire (scalding)
  Ban the pan (hot fat for cooking)
  Smoking causes cancer (cigarettes)
  Quit for life! (cigarettes)
  Rat on a rat – drug dealers ruin lives (hard drugs)
  Speed kills (dangerous driving)

▲ *Good information and open discussion, whether at school or at home, can help young people to make better decisions in life.*

Find similar slogans, or write your own. What do you think makes a slogan successful? Do slogans make you stop and think about the risks of certain activities?

Although gambling is also a risky activity, few governments have education campaigns about the dangers of gambling. In fact, most slogans have been developed by the gambling industry. Critics say that these slogans are not nearly as educational or hard-hitting as they should be.

▼ *'Gambling – it's a dog's life!' Can you think of another slogan for this picture which could warn people against gambling?*

Here are some slogans used by betting shops and casinos.

♦ Have fun, but play it safe
♦ Bet with your head, not above it
♦ Gambling can be addictive
♦ If it's no fun, walk away
♦ If you play with real dollars, play with real sense

Do you think these slogans really warn people about the risks and dangers of gambling? Can you think of better slogans or better ways to educate people?

GLOSSARY

Addiction
When a person cannot stop doing something, even when it is harmful.

Betting
Placing money on the result of an event.

Betting shops
Special shops where people can place bets.

Casino
A place where gambling takes place, with card games, roulette and electronic gaming machines.

Credit card
A plastic card which allows a person to borrow money.

Cyberspace
The world of electronic communication.

Debt
Money owed to another person or organization.

Depressed
When a person feels that life is worthless.

Discriminates
When a person treats someone else unfairly or unequally.

Draw
Choosing an item at random.

Electronic gaming machine
Machines played by inserting coins, then pressing buttons or pulling a lever. A winning pattern brings a payout.

Fruit machine
An electronic gaming machine with a low payout.

Hooked
A common way of describing an addiction.

Illegal
Against the law.

Internet
The worldwide electronic information system.

Jackpot
The major prize in a lottery.

Laws of probability
Mathematical rules that predict the likelihood of an event taking place.

Legal
Allowed by the law.

Log on
Starting a computer or entering a website.

Lottery
A random draw with a chance to win a prize.

Odds
The likelihood of a result or an event taking place.

On-line
Doing something through a computer.

Poker machines
A common name for electronic gaming machines.

Professional
Earning money from an activity, instead of just doing it as a hobby.

Random
A chance happening.

Re-mortgage
A second loan on a house.

Roulette
A game played on a table with a revolving centre over which a ball runs.

Slogans
Short messages.

Slot machine
A common name for electronic gaming machines.

Sociable
Enjoying company, friendly.

Social security
A payment made by the government to a person who is not able to work.

Status
The place a person occupies in the eyes of other people.

Stress
Pressure, worry.

Syndicate
A group who join together for a common purpose.

Taxes
Money paid to the government.

Virtual
Often used to refer to something created by computers which is not real.

Website
Information on a particular topic that is available on the Internet.

ORGANIZATIONS

Worldwide there are organizations providing information and advice about gambling. The organizations below can supply educational material and resources. Information is also available on the Internet.

Australia

Australian Council of Social Service
Locked Bag 11
Darlinghurst, NSW 2010

Australian Institute
of Gambling Research
University of Western Sydney,
Macarthur, PO Box 555
Campbelltown, NSW, 2560

Victoria Council
on Problem Gambling
Level 2, 153 Park Street
South Melbourne, Victoria, 3205

Canada

Canadian Centre
on Substance Abuse
75 Albert St, Suite 300
Ottawa, Ontario, K1P 5E7
Website: www.ccsa.ca

Canadian Foundation on
Compulsive Gambling (Ontario)
Website:
www.responsiblegambling.org

UK

GAMCARE
Suite 1, Catherine House
25–27 Catherine Place
London SW1E 6DU
Tel: 020 7233 8988
Website: www.gamcare.org.uk

USA

California Council
on Problem Gambling
121 South Palm Drive, Suite 202
Palm Springs, California 92262
Website:
www.calproblemgambling.org

Gamblers Anonymous
Website:
www.gamblersanonymous.org

North American Training Institute
314 W. Superior Street, Suite 702
Duluth, Minnesota 55802
Website: www.nati.org

RESOURCES

A Certain Bet – Exploring Gambling?
(GAMCARE, 1997)
Aims to help teenagers to make informed choices and to gamble responsibly. Price: £15 plus £3 p&p. Available from GAMCARE.

Australia's Gambling Industries, Productivity Commission, December 1999
A detailed government report available from their website: www.pc.gov.au/inquiry/gambling/

Essential Articles 5: The Resource File for Issues,
(Carel Press, 1999)
A collection of articles covering 157 topics with several articles on the benefits and problems of gambling in the UK.
Available from: Carel Press, 4 Hewson Street, Carlisle, CA2 5AU, UK

Gambling: Issues for the Nineties, Vol. 78
by Kaye Healey,
(The Spinney Press, 1997)
Articles on gambling in Australia, covering benefits and problems of gambling, and government and community attitudes. Available from: The Spinney Press, 226 Darling Street, Balmain, NSW, 2041, Australia. Price: $14.50 plus p&p.

National Gambling Impact Study Commission, June 1999
A detailed government report on gambling in the USA. Available from their website: www.ngisc.gov

Stone Cold by Pete Hautman (School and Library Binding, 1998)
Novel about a teenage gambler in the USA and his ups and downs with gambling.

Wanna Bet?
A cool magazine for teens concerned about gambling, North American Training Institute.
An on-line magazine, regularly updated, for and by young people, with activities and feedback.
Website: www.wannabet.org

NB. Most gambling websites are commercial, not educational.

INDEX